THE FABULOUS LOST & FOUND

AND THE LITTLE NORWEGIAN MOUSE

WRITTEN BY MARK PALLIS
ILLUSTRATED BY PETER BAYNTON

NEU WESTEND
— PRESS —

For Emily and Lucy - MP

For Lotte and Finn - PB

THE FABULOUS LOST & FOUND AND THE LITTLE NORWEGIAN MOUSE
Copyright text © 2020 Mark Pallis and Copyright images © 2020 Peter Baynton

First Printing, April 2020
ISBN: 978-1-913595-10-4
NeuWestendPress.com

THE FABULOUS LOST & FOUND

AND THE LITTLE NORWEGIAN MOUSE

WRITTEN BY MARK PALLIS
ILLUSTRATED BY PETER BAYNTON

NEU WESTEND
— PRESS —

In the middle of the big city is a tiny
yellow building. If anyone loses anything, this is
where it ends up.

It is called the Lost and Found.

Mr and Mrs Frog keep everything safe, hoping that someday every lost watch and bag and phone and toy and shoe and cheesegrater will find its owner again.

But the shop is very small. And there are so many lost things. It is all quite a squeeze, but still, it's fabulous.

One sunny day, a little mouse walked in.

"Welcome," said Mrs Frog. "What have you lost?"

"Jeg har mistet lua mi," said the mouse.

Mr and Mrs Frog could not speak Norwegian. They had no idea what the little mouse was saying.

What shall we do? they wondered.

Maybe she's lost an umbrella. Everyone loses an umbrella at least twice, thought Mr Frog.

"Have you lost this?" asked Mr Frog.

"En paraply? Nei," replied the mouse.

Then Mrs Frog remembered something
that had been handed in a few months ago...

"Is this yours?" Mrs Frog asked, holding up a chunk of cheese.

"Ost? Nei. Den stinker!" said the mouse.

"Time to put that cheese in the bin dear," said Mr Frog.

"Maybe the word 'lue' means coat," said Mr Frog.

"Now where did I put that nice
yellow one?"

"Got it!" said Mr Frog.

"En jakke? Nei. Jeg har mistet lua mi," said the mouse.

She was starting to feel a bit frustrated.

"We need to keep trying," said Mrs Frog.

Ikke et skjerf.

Ikke bukser.

Ikke en genser.

Ikke solbriller.

Ikke sko.

"Jeg har mistet lua mi,"
said the mouse.

Ikke to sykler.

Ikke en datamaskin.

Ikke tre bøker.

Ikke fire bananer.

Ikke fem nøkler.

It was no good. A fat wet tear rolled
down the mouse's cheek.

"How about a nice cup of tea?" asked Mrs Frog kindly.

"Ja gjerne, jeg elsker te. Takk," replied the mouse. They sat together, sipping their tea and all feeling a bit sad.

Suddenly, the mouse realised she could try pointing.

She pointed at her head.
"Lue!" she said.

"I've got it!" exclaimed Mrs Frog, leaping up.

"A wig of course!" said Mrs Frog.

"Nei ikke en parykk," said the mouse.

Ikke rød.

Ikke blond.

Ikke brun.

Ikke grønn.

Ikke flerfarget.

"What about this?"
asked Mr Frog, pulling back
a curtain.

"Lue!" exclaimed the
mouse.

"Ah, so a 'lue' is a hat.
Wonderful!" Mr and Mrs
Frog cheered.

For høy.

For liten.

For stram.

For stor.

"One hat left," said Mrs Frog, reaching all the way to the back of the cupboard.

"It couldn't be this old thing, could it?"

"Lua mi.

Jeg har funnet lua mi!

Tusen takk," said the mouse.

And just like that, the mouse found her hat.

"Ha det bra," she said, as she skipped away.
"Ha det bra," replied Mr and Mrs Frog.

"I wonder who will come tomorrow?" said Mr Frog.
Mrs Frog put her arm around him.

"I don't know," she replied, giving him a squeeze,
"but whoever it is, we'll do our best to help."

LEARNING TO LOVE LANGUAGES

An additional language opens a child's mind, broadens their horizons and enriches their emotional life. Research has shown that the time between a child's birth and their sixth or seventh birthday is a "golden period" when they are most receptive to new languages. This is because they have an in-built ability to distinguish the sounds they hear and make sense of them. The Story-powered Language Learning Method taps into these natural abilities.

HOW THE STORY-POWERED LANGUAGE LEARNING METHOD WORKS

We create an emotionally engaging and funny story for children and adults to enjoy together, just like any other picture book. Studies show that social interaction, like enjoying a book together, is critical in language learning.

Through the story, we introduce a relatable character who speaks only in the new language. This helps build empathy and a positive attitude towards people who speak different languages. These are both important aspects in laying the foundations for lasting language acquisition in a child's life.

As the story progresses, the child naturally works with the characters to discover the meanings of a wide range of fun new words. Strategic use of humour ensures that this subconscious learning is rewarded with laughter; the child feels good and the first seeds of a lifelong love of languages are sown.

For more information and free downloads visit www.neuwestendpress.com

ALL THE BEAUTIFUL NORWEGIAN WORDS AND PHRASES FROM OUR STORY

Jeg har mistet lua mi	I've lost my hat
paraply	umbrella
ost	cheese
den stinker	it stinks
jakke	coat
skjerf	scarf
bukser	trousers
solbriller	sunglasses
genser	sweater
sko	shoes
en	one
to	two
tre	three
fire	four
fem	five
datamaskin	computer
bøker	books
nøkler	keys
bananer	bananas
sykler	bicycles
gjerne	happily
Jeg elsker te	I love tea
takk	thanks
tusen takk	thank you
parykk	wig
rød	red
blond	blond
brun	brown
grønn	green
flerfarget	multicoloured
nei	no
for høy	too tall
for stor	too big
for liten	too small
for stram	too tight
jeg har funnet lua mi	I've found my hat
ha det bra	goodbye

THE WORLD OF
THE FABULOUS LOST & FOUND

THIS STORY IS ALSO AVAILABLE IN...

FRENCH

SPANISH

ITALIAN

CZECH

KOREAN

WELSH

GERMAN

HEBREW

SWEDISH

POLISH

SLOVAKIAN

VIETNAMESE

LATIN

PORTUGUESE

...AND MANY MORE LANGUAGES!

ENJOYED IT?
WRITE A REVIEW AND
LET US KNOW!

@MARK_PALLIS ON TWITTER
WWW.MARKPALLIS.COM

@PETERBAYNTON ON INSTAGRAM
WWW.PETERBAYNTON.COM

Made in the USA
Coppell, TX
08 May 2022

77560964R10024